THE
OVERSEER

The Overseer

Copyright © 2012, C. Sterling Davis, II

ISBN: 10: 0615767427

ISBN: 13: 978-0615767420 (C. Sterling Davis, II)

DEDICATION

This book is dedicated to
the life and legacy of my mother

SYLVIA LEE WILBORNS

JULY 2, 1941 – NOVEMBER 2, 2002

See You Later...

Special Thanks To...

The precious gifts of God to me; Alesia Len, Kha'ryn Aleyah, C. Sterling, III and Trinity Sterlynn! Thank you for your love, patience and support during this endeavor. I love you all more than you could ever imagine.

To one of the strongest women I know. Whose support, persistence and passionate pushing into purpose has been a constant in my life and ministry; thank you for believing in me when I didn't believe in myself. I LOVE YOU...

Beulah Clarise Davis

AUTHOR'S NOTE

His Grace J. Delano Ellis, II, the Metropolitan Arch Bishop of the Joint College of African Pentecostal Bishops states that the commission of "The College" is:

  a. Provide training and tools for leadership with a view to the Bishopric.

  b. Protecting the Episcopacy and assuring that it conforms to orthodoxy as to weed out the unsuitable and pretenders to the chair.

  c. Prepare episcopal candidates beyond commitment to Christ, divine calling and theological preparation; to develop in them a high moral content of character with a strong emphasis on family.

As the Overseer is the foundation of the episcopacy (epi – over, skopos – to see) the above stated commission should start with the lower house of the prelature to ensure purity in the prelature with success in the line of succession.

There are many Overseers that attend "The College" and other varied trainings and symposiums and have confessed that they are "unclear" and "unsure" of their role; philosophically and functionally within confines of their communes. Though each commune or fellowship regards the office of the Overseer very valuable to their success, the assumption is that the appointed cleric should have "some idea" as to what the office entails and how to function. This ambiguity causes great instability not just in the office but, the OFFICER!

The larger context is that, if there instability in the lower house, the evolution of the "good bishop" is surely in peril.

Within this dispensation of time, the episcopate has become "faddish" and diluted because of the illegitimate means, methods and modes by which Arch Bishops, Bishops, Apostles and even Overseers have proliferated onto the canvas of the ecclesia. Most not knowing the richness of the history and the great bond to the order and standards of Christ and His Church! This is not about exalted positions, excessive pageantry, extensive exercises…this is about executing in excellence and exactness of the dignity and legacy of the offices that govern the Bride and Her affairs. It's about the lives that depend on the content and the character of those that are the chief contenders and defenders of the faith. Not the pretenders and offenders!

With the priests that have been called and confirmed into the lower house of the prelature, the purity of the journey for the next generation of prelates begins with this in mind.

It is to that end that this treatise is written.

Vero Quod Muneris,
(In Truth and Service)

C. Sterling Davis, II +
Overseer
The Renaissance Covenantal Consortium and
Senior Pastor of The Renaissance Church of Houston

TABLE OF CONTENTS

CHAPTER 1
THE HISTORICAL OVERSEER

The bishops of the early church (and still today) govern the affairs of the church, and to establish systems, offices, and positions that ensure the effective and efficient administration of the church.

With such a vast and expansive purview, the episcopacy has had great need of those who could support the office in the manifestation of vision, administration and governance. For centuries in the church different levels of the prelature have been instituted to delegate duties and accomplish objectives; although, not all levels of the prelature are reserved for those of episcopal rank. The term prelate is derived from the Latin word "prelatus" meaning "one preferred" in our context it simply means one of high ranking ecclesiastical authority.

We find strong evidence that the office of the Overseer, as we know it today, has a historical origin of sorts in the Roman Rite of the Catholic Church, and is a hybrid of the Papal Honors that were bestowed upon the clergy. When this tremendous honor was conferred upon a member of the clergy they became a member of the "prelaturae gratiae" or Prelature of Grace/Honor (Honorary Prelature).

The honorary prelature was considered the lower-ranking, non-episcopal house, which is to say that the authority of this house was not autonomous and the clerics did not carry succession as did the "regular" episcopates. Ergo, many of these posts are held by priests without episcopal dignity, but due to the nature of their appointment or recognition, are being deemed capable of greater responsibility and as such, greater honor.

The foundational facet in the history of the Overseer starts with the position commonly known as Monsignor. For a short time in the 14th century, the Papal Court operated out of Avignon, France. During that time in France, those clerics/priests who worked in the Papal executive/administrative offices (known as the Curia) were addressed as "Monseigneur" (Monsignor) meaning "my lord".

The term Monsignor actually addresses a number of special appointments made by the Pope, or acknowledging a priest's service to the church and/or Papal office. The majority of these titles were initially granted as being personal or domestic in nature as the residency of these clerics were in Rome.

As a result of being awarded with such honor, these clerics were allowed to adorn some of the Episcopal Vesture and be addressed in the official style of "Right Reverend Monsignor" or "Very Reverend Monsignor" dependent upon their ranking/designation in the lower house of the prelature. This was one of the fundamental Papal Honors that were granted and as such there were varying degrees of the Monsignor. Within the Monsignori there were sixteen different positions that existed prior to the Pontificalis Domus (The Papal Household) decree of 1969 given by the hand of Pope Paul VI.

This motu proprio (meaning on his own impulse/accord) was given in order to bring the church into a more pastoral mode of operations and governance. Of the Monsignor positions, the most closely related to our Protestant Overseer is that of the Prelate of Honor/Domestic Prelate. The title Domestic Prelate was given prior to the Pontificalis Domus and was renamed as the Prelate of Honor. Prior to the Papal decree there were two distinct Domestic Prelates; the greater prelates and the lesser prelates (honorary). The greater prelates were awarded episcopal dignity. This entitled them to have voice in the Roman Curia and the Papal Court.

They were non-Oriental patriarchs, the archbishops and bishops who had senior positions in Papal Chapel as deans, auditors and the like. These positions of governance were not given to the lesser house; they assisted the greater house in the execution of the aforementioned duties.

Within the sixteen positions of the Monsignori, there existed sixteen different honors that could be awarded to the priests. Of the sixteen, the lesser house honors were the most frequently awarded. This title was granted for life to the cleric without specificity of responsibility in Rome or within a diocese.

The duties for this particular position were "fluid" in that based on the need and their specific expertise, they were given their assignments and these could change or be added to request of a diocesan bishop, Curia or the Pope. These clerics are chosen by the Pope to carry out special functions within their diocese or specific area/specialty to support the work and objectives of the Papacy. Persons who have been given this honor receive a nomination letter from the Vatican Secretariat of State and their title is not valid until the date is applied to the sealed bulla in Rome.

The nomination announcement of the Prelato d'Onore di Sua Santita (The Prelate of Honor of His Holiness) is usually executed simultaneously with the group of other papal honors being conferred at that time within a diocese.

The legacy of the Prelate of Honor or Domestic Prelate is upheld by the office of the modern day Protestant Overseer. The Overseer, like the Prelate of Honor/Domestic Prelate, is given the honor to serve his or her commune, fellowship or reformation by recommendation of their diocesan bishop or the Presiding Prelate. This cleric ultimately works to support the office of the Presiding Prelate directly on the national/international level, which is solely determined by the Cathedra or indirectly at the diocesan level under the authority of the diocesan bishop.

Though they carry episcopal ranking, their authority is not inherent nor autonomous but derived from (and subject to/controlled by) the Presiding Prelate or the Diocesan Bishop. The only such case that the Overseer has "autonomy" is in the case of the General Overseer. This title is given to one that sits as the head of a fellowship and is granted that position by election of those that submit to their authority.

The General Overseer, in some cases doesn't have episcopal dignity, but has complete autonomy as they are the establishmentarian. This title is also shared but, not to be confused with the Presiding Bishop. The Presiding Bishop of a fellowship, commune or reformation, may chose to use this title as well, but again they are consecrated bishops with full episcopal dignity, inclusive of Apostolic Succession.

The episcopacy is the highest level of ecclesiastical service, and as such should be safe guarded from the novice, the ill-prepared, the spiritually, and academically unqualified. Therefore, oversight of special areas of ministry are placed under the purview of priests who have shown potential to effectively and efficiently administrate and lead, whose character, competency can hold the weight of the responsibility of this office.

Just as the Prelates of Honor, the Overseer has not been awarded episcopal dignities, other than the prescribed vestments (which we will discuss in a later chapter), the right to be addressed in the official style of "The Very Reverend..." and to use the sign of the cross at the end of their signature. Please note, that the sign of the cross is placed at the beginning of the Bishop's signature.

Though the history of the overseer finds it's genesis in the womb of the mother church, it doesn't end there. In the facets of the protestant reformations, we find various offices of oversight that are not commonly known as overseers. The following are just a few of the names given to overseers in the respective denominations:

Church Of God In Christ – District Superintendent

African Methodist Episcopal Church – Presiding Elders/District Elders

Christian Methodist Episcopal Church – Presiding Elders/District Elders

Pentecostal Assemblies of the World – Suffragan Bishop

Baptist Church – Moderator

Presbyterian Church – Ruling Elder

Anglican Church - Vicar General

Again, these are just a few of the names that are ascribed as overseers in their respective denominations. Though the names are different, the functionality is still the same. It is to assist their leader(s) in the furthering of their influence and vision on the local and national level.

From the Monsignor to the modern day Overseer, one thing is certain; that the sanctity of serving in the lower house of the prelature is one of high honor.

CHAPTER 2

THE BIBLICAL OVERSEER

Though the office of Overseer has a rich historical foundation, the origin of that foundation is found in the Holy Writ. History gives us the shell of the office while the Bible gives us the substance of the appointment.

One of the earliest accounts of oversight is of course found in Genesis 1:28 – 31, 2:8,9, 15-17 and the 3rd Chapter. It is not that we liken the Presiding Prelate or the Diocesan Bishop to God, but in this context we find that the Bishop functions like God in relation to Adam and the Overseer respectively.

In the onset of the relationship God gives Adam authority (dominion) to rule, but not without parameters. Authority didn't inherently or naturally exist with Adam, it existed with God and He delegated it to him. Adams' (male and female) authority came from God and the substratum of their power came from them being made in the image and likeness of God; which is to say that Adam's rule wasn't completely autonomous; He had to rule the earth as God would, he has to make decisions as God would make them!

The scope of Adam's authority is bound to the fact that he is made in the image and likeness of God. It is here that Adam learns the first rule of oversight here in Genesis; that of delegated authority.

In delegated authority, the individual has to recognize three realities:

1. The Overseer's authority is not independent of their Bishop.

2. The authority of the overseer doesn't equate to ownership.

3. The Overseer must accurately represent (re-present) the source in order to extend the influence of the source.

To fully understand the dependency of authority within delegated authority, we look to Genesis. In the case of Adam, his promotion from clay to the crown of creation was nestled in the declaration of God. Without that defining declaration and functional formation he would not have existed as we know him! He would have simply been dust and dirt with no dominion, just a common part of the domain. Adam is who he is and has what he has ALL because God delegated His authority! Herein lies the same basic principle that the Overseer must remember. Your elevation to the office is SOLEY due to your Bishop! While we understand that promotion/elevation comes from God, He uses people in authority to confirm and confer upon those that He has chosen. (1 Sam 16)

This is one of the fundamental facts that must not be overlooked. God will NEVER circumvent authority figures to elevate you. This same scenario is seen in the succession of our Savior. Jesus' elevation is only declared from heaven after His submission to John. (Matt 3) It is noteworthy to mention that even after this and sometime thereafter, people were still avid followers of John and not Jesus. They came to John and took issue with Jesus' baptismal authority. It was John's affirmation to his followers that served as validation for the authority of Christ. (John 3:25-36) In the above referenced text, Jesus was well into doing ministry and had amassed a following and his own disciples, but the larger contingency was still John's followers. Herein lies another truth within this context of where authority rests; no matter how great of a leader, preacher and administrator you are, there are those that will not relinquish their loyalty and allegiance to you without the leaders validation of you. The psychology behind it is steeped in their relationship with the leader and the effect that the leader has had in their lives. Before there was a "you" there was the leader. The leader that cared for them taught them and even disciplined them. But, was an intricate part of the fabric of their lives.

Just because you show up and are good at what you do and you have the title and the authority doesn't necessarily give the influence and subsequent "buy in" from the people. This transition of power via delegation not only takes time but, moreover it takes validation.

Part of the leader's validation comes through your submission but is accompanied by your open recognition of whom the leader is in relation to you and the appointment given. Jesus often esteems John publicly, knowing that where He is and where He is going, was initiated by the authority and validation of the one that preceded Him in establishing the way; John. As Overseers, you must never cease to confirm your allegiance and loyalty to your leader in the eyes and ears of those in your charge for therein lays the secret to your influence and possible elevation.

As we look to explore our second reality, we have to conclude, in retrospect; Adams' elevation and authority came through the declaration of God. Nowhere in that declaration did God relinquish His ownership. Adam was given dominion over, fish, fowl, the fields and the beasts. He was given dominion NOT ownership.

This is to say that Adam couldn't do what he wanted to do with that which he was given charge over. Because, he was made in the image and likeness of God, the expectation was that he would be in earth what God is to both heaven and earth. His image and likeness were the boundaries of his decision-making and his responses to issues had there been any. The thought is you can't have complete autonomy when you are not the owner. It is David who underwrites God's ownership of everything in his penning of Psalm 24:1. So, at best Adam is a leader under authority.

As is Adam in the Genesis account, so is the Overseer in their reformations, fellowships and communes; leaders under authority and those that have dominion, but not ownership. The ownership rests in the source of the one who is delegating the authority. In Adam's case it was God and in the case of the Overseer it is the Bishop. This ownership is not based in a proprietary sense in this case. This ownership is more so on the lines of ultimate amenability.

As the Bishop, presiding prelate, diocesan or otherwise, the weight of liability rests on them and NOT the Overseer. From the fiscal to the administrative, legally and spiritually it is the ranking episcopates that are ultimately held responsible for the governance of the "fellows" and the "ship". Their accountability reaches from the throne of God, to seats in government and even the chairs in the homes of those that they are called to serve.

This is not to disregard and make light of the duties and responsibilities of the Overseer. It is to say that the Overseer has to walk a very delicate albeit fine line in their scope of authority. One of the greatest dangers in one having authority is thinking that they are the authority. Remember, the authority that is possessed is that of delegated authority; meaning that even the authority possessed is not owned by the individual. Therefore, if the authority is delegated and not owned then that which is under the authority of the delegate is not owned. With this in mind, the Overseer has to govern themselves accordingly in demeanor, decisions and duties. Though the assignment is "owned" by the Overseer, the carrying out and even ultimately the success is not COMPLETELY their own.

In the forefront of the Overseer's mind they should be thinking about how their leader would handle a situation and what would be the best course of action as to not bring any undue embarrassment, tension or weight to the leader and the organization. This mindset is not to rob them of their individuality and uniqueness of opinion and/or thought. But, it is to discipline the individual's thoughts and behaviors until such time that they are elevated and the expansion of the kingdom via the reformation or fellowship is in their hands as the authority.

This discipline of demeanor, decision and duty helps them in this event of elevation not veer too far from the foundation upon which the organization was established which leaves the legacy of the establishmentarian intact and this enables the original intent of God for the fellowship/reformation to continue until the day of Christ's return as it is deemed a "good work" that has begun. Again, this is not to say that the individuality of the Overseer is not wanted or warranted it is to say that the unique gifting and intelligence of the Overseer is bound to the scope of the leaders vision. The expectation is that the relationship between the two is a synergistic one at best.

As the Overseer submits their gifts, talents and intelligence to the organization and it's leadership with the intent to optimize it's influence, effectiveness and efficiency, that the organization and it's leadership will in turn use that increased influence, effectiveness and efficiency to enlarge and expand the agenda/vision of the Overseer and their local congregation and personal ministry endeavors. As this relationship stays in this synergistic vein and the roles and intents remain pure and not based in politics, position, pretense and payment, then success and proper succession will be inevitable.

The final consideration is an intricate part in the success of succession is rooted in the Overseer's ability to represent (re-present) his leader to the fullest extent possible. In representing the leader correctly there are a couple of things to consider that are paramount for success:

1. That true representation of authority is not devoid of possessing authority.

2. That all authority needs to be assessed to ensure accurate representation.

In the first point, God's declaration of delegation is found in the statement "and let him have dominion…" This declaration could be understood to say that man could've have just been made in His image and likeness alone and quite possibly NOT had dominion (authority) until he proved that he could handle it. But, this is not the case at all. God knew that in order to have a true representation of Himself that He would have to "grant" man dominion. Now, this dominion was not given to him for any other reason than to be on the earth that which He was in heaven and earth! That is to say that all Adam was given dominion to do was to be God's executor in the earth and rule it like He would. Minus the authority, Adam would have been just like the other beasts, plant life and elements; something that exists under authority with NO authority.

This point yields houses another point that speaks to the heart of this "dominion factor". That ultimate authority rests in the ability to choose! The only thing that Adam had that NOTHING else had was the ability to choose. Birds have no choice in what they are going to do for the winter; Bears can't decide to stay up for the winter; Animals can't choose when to mate, etc. Man's authority rests in him having that ability!

But, TRUE authority rests in his ability to decide like God what God would decide, thus making him (man) truly "like" God.

Overseers, have to keep this very thing in the forefront of their minds; that the authority given to them is not for them to be them, but for them to be the physical representation of their leader in their area of authority. More specifically, to make the decisions that the leader would make with the welfare of the commune in mind and not to fulfill a self-aggrandizing need based on position, politics and power. Using the authority given, to make right representational decisions is the highest form of respect and honor given to a leader by those that he/she has delegated. The saying goes that "imitation is best form of flattery". This means that in order to imitate someone, you have taken the time to study them, learn their mannerisms, phraseology, etc. So, the better or more accurate the imitation (re-presentation) of the individual shows how meticulous you were in the study and that is a compliment to who the person is, in that you would study them to such a degree as to NOT misrepresent them.

Overseers, study your leaders in order to maximize the authority given to you. Before there is "many" there is the management of the "few". Meaning, that before you are given complete autonomy in the "many" decisions that have to be made, you have represent well in the "few" decisions that you have to make, in light of the fact that you are making them in the "spirit of your leader".

In the maximization process of this authority there has to be "quality control" to ensure accuracy. This is not accuracy just for accuracy's sake. But, this accuracy is for the safeguarding of what is to be as well!

To better understand this we have to go back to God's relationship with Adam. More succinctly found in the Adam's first exercise of authority; the nomenclature of the beasts. If you look carefully at the fore noted scripture, you will see that Adam's work was overseen by God and then confirmed by God. God brought the beasts to Adam, "to see" what he would call them and then God confirmed it. This denotes that if Adam was inaccurate in the exercise of nomenclature, then God would have stepped in and either guided him through correction or would have just corrected it Himself.

Either way, He oversaw the process as to ensure accuracy and even larger to protect the future and functionality of the beasts. Imagine a cow being called a chicken? The cow would be trying to lay eggs instead of giving milk and cluck instead of moo...it would have been a disaster! So, God had to supervise the situation in order to have accurate representation and to ensure proper functionality of that which had authority and that which was under authority. Though the Bishop has given you authority to re-present him in the area of authority given, supervision is still necessary. Just as in the text, God supervised (super – over, vision – to see) Adam in his new role. Adam was new to the role of being God's emissary in the earth and needed supervision whether he knew it or not.

Just as Adam is new to this role of emissary, some of you are new to this role as well. Even those of you that have been in this awhile, this is either a refresher for you or a new concept in your role as Overseer. Either way, in the infancy of this role, supervision is necessary to ensure that you as the Overseer are making the proper decisions.

This again, is not to say that you lack the intelligence to do this, moreover, it is a way that the Bishop has a chance to assess your decision making process in order to protect his/her investment of promotion.

Your leaders WANT you to do well! They want you to succeed! They want to eventually be able to consecrate you as Bishop! So, they're supervising you as a way to ensure that the decision to promote you is secured and that you are on the right path.

his counsel should be received in accordance to the following Proverbs:

1.   Proverbs 1:5

2.   Proverbs 12:15

3.   Proverbs 15:22

4.   Proverbs 19:20

These, and other proverbial sayings of Solomon are paramount for the Overseer if he/she is to be successful.

In this supervision, the Overseer also has to keep in mind what's at stake; the health and growth of the commune/fellowship! Ergo, the Bishop has to make sure that in your decision making that things are "defined" and "named" properly to protect purpose and functionality of that which is in your purview.

The extreme of the aforementioned is the issue of micromanaging or premature autonomy. Micro - managing should be understood by the Overseer NOT as an accusation of ignorance, but as a proving ground of trust and competence to your leader. Your Bishop has a tremendous burden of leadership on his/her shoulders and with that there are persons who attach themselves to him/her for different reasons. It is for this reason, among others that they are very cautious and sometimes this causes issues in trust. So, micromanaging is the secondary consequence of such experiences and is NOT to be taken personally.

Premature autonomy usually happens when the leader's agenda and/or plate is too full. This can also occur, when there is no training or accountability process in place. Being released completely into a situation without supervision is not always a badge of honor; this can sometimes backfire into beast of burden. Proper supervision upfront may seem expensive but, without the supervision, it will be more expensive on the back end! Preventive maintenance is always less expensive than repair.

Another reference that gives great credence to the issue of representation of the leader is found in Numbers 11:16,17. God tells Moses to take the leaders/officers that he has appointed to the tent of meeting and there He will take the spirit that is on Moses and give it to the leaders. This is done to assist Moses in the carrying of the weight of leadership. Now, the basis of this transference was steeped in the fact that Moses couldn't be everywhere at the same time and there needed to be the same level of leadership, care and concern for the people. So, God took the ruach that was on Moses and places it on them. This is God "replicating" Moses' mind, motives, heart, perception and perspectives in the leaders; basically making them "Lil' Moses'" to lead them as he would even when he couldn't be present physically. This enabled them to assist Moses to carry the burden of the people "accurately" so as not to misguide them in their own individuality and possible misinterpretation of their leader Moses. This is the passage where we get the colloquialism, "carrying the spirit of your leader".

As Overseers you must receive an impartation from your leader to be a leader! This text helps to further drive the point that it is vital to be the embodiment of your leader to and for the people. Your body, your leader's voice; your eyes, your leader's vision and insight; your brain, your leader's thoughts.

The Overseer must remember that the authority given is for the purpose of carrying out the vision of the leader concerning the commune and not that of ones drive and desire for power and prestige. The second reason for this authority is to empower the Overseer to be a direct reflection of their leader through representation. Therefore causing the leader's influence to be indirectly felt through the presence and persona of the Overseer.

In doing so, you will never be guilty of hubris as you will undoubtedly know that you have the distinct honor and privilege of representing your leader.

CHAPTER 3

CREDENTIALS AND CHARACTER

As a member of the prelature, albeit the "lower house" but the prelature nonetheless, the Overseer has to be just as sound as those that are of episcopal dignity. Sound in their theology points and thought processes and sound in the content and constitution of their character. These are two major "building blocks in the foundation of the Overseer, especially as it pertains to the life and legacy of the commune in which they are called to serve.

Metropolitan Archbishop J. Delano Ellis, II, the Chair and President Bishop of the Joint College of African American Pentecostal Bishops and the Presiding Bishop of the Pentecostal Churches of Christ, states that, "The very first steps beyond commitment to Christ, divine calling and theological preparation for a candidate must be in them a very high moral content of character with a strong emphasis on family!" Though this statement is directed toward those candidates for episcopal consideration, it should not start at the moment of candidacy; it should be the preparatory hallmark for the Overseer.

Jude, the brother of James writes and urges the saints to "earnestly contend for the faith which was once for all handed down to the saints." The phrasing "earnestly contend for" is taken from the transliterated word epagónizomai which is to contend (literally, "struggle upon, appropriately"), i.e. with skill and commitment in opposing whatever is not of the faith. The operative word for this context is "skill". Between The Metropolitan and Jude it is clear that the Overseer needs to have more than just a commitment to Christ, His Church and call, there has to be competency.

The Overseer's credentialing is vitally important for a myriad of reasons. The initial licensure and ordination are the bedrocks of the elevation to the lower house of the prelature. The hope is that the catechism for ordination was thorough and done properly as to ascertain that beyond the individual's gifting that there is an understanding of the Tenets of the Faith, the call to eldership, the doctrine of the church/reformation, protocol and liturgy (especially concerning the ordinances of the church). The overseer cannot assist in the matters of church polity, policy nor could he/she police the aforementioned without some degree of learning beyond that of the Holy Scriptures.

Also, this is an office of administration! Business matters are part of the purview of the Overseer. Though the reformation/commune is NOT asking for an MBA, the priest in this position should have some business acumen attached to their portfolio. The larger note for consideration is that, if the abovementioned is not possessed, the DESIRE to accumulate the knowledge SHOULD BE! The cleric should want to be well informed, well read and well versed enough to be an asset to the vision, to the church and to the Body of Christ globally!

To better understand the necessary skills as it pertains to the ecclesia in relation to the episcopal order let's look at the Dreyfus Model of Skills Acquisition Stages:

Office	Stage	Description
Minister In Training	Novice	Rigid adherence to taught rules or plans Little situational perception No discretionary judgment
Licensed Minister	Advanced Beginner	Guidelines for action based on attributes or aspects. Situational perception still limited All attributes and aspects are treated separately and given equal importance
Ordained Elder	Competent	Coping with "crowdedness" Now sees actions at least partly in terms of longer-term goals Conscious deliberate planning Standardized and routinized procedures
Overseer	Proficient	Sees situations holistically rather than in terms of aspects

		Sees what is most important in a situation Perceives deviations from the normal pattern Decision-making less labored Uses maxims for guidance, whose meaning varies according to the situation
Bishop	Expert	No longer relies on rules, guidelines or maxims Intuitive grasp of situations based on deep tacit understanding Analytic approaches used only in novel situations or when problems occur Vision of what is possible

The Overseer is proficient! Their proficiency rests in the acquisition of the necessary skill set theologically, logistically, financially and administratively.

Jude speaks of this proficiency as "contenders" on the theological side. The cycle of life and culture brings to bear that the same issues that caused Jude to write are the same that are facing the church today!

In this "information age", people are more intelligent and informed. The unfortunate reality is that most of them are more biblically astute than most clerics. Also, hedonistic mindsets that lead to decadent lifestyles are the leading factors in the decay of the moral fibers and the societal fabric. So to that end, it behooves the Overseer to be sound in their theology and doctrine as to be able to articulate the truths of the Holy Writ with depth of skill.

Again, this level of development (proficient) is quite necessary not just to contend for the faith but, to also extend the kingdom. In this modernity, it takes more than a "whoop and a holla" accompanied by "rhymes and rhetoric", there has to be a sound theological acumen that becomes the catalyst for the "renewing of the mind" for the saint and sinner alike.

It is the blend of knowledge in the sacred and the secular that allow for the Overseer to not just articulate the faith, but it also becomes the cornerstone of their "prophetic voice". This prophetic voice becomes the vehicle whereby they can then speak "truth to power" in civic and political arenas. It is Paul who's academic pedigree allows him the wherewithal to speak to King Agrippa in such a manner that the King had to testify to that Paul almost persuaded him to be a Christian.

In like fashion, the Overseer has to be able to move through the ranks of society being "wise as a serpent, yet harmless as a dove" while being the manifested prayer of Solomon being wise enough to "move in and out amongst the people". This happened not by eloquence but, education.

The Overseer should either possess or be in pursuit of sound, accredited, sacred and secular learning. From basic business and accounting to systematic theology, homiletics and hermeneutics these among others are the essence of what is needed to be equipped to equip. With varying doctrines from the diverse denominations, erroneous claims from "minstrel-esque" ministerial money-making machines to the plethora of heresies that are proliferating on the scene from the lips of prophets, preachers and pontiffs, one needs to be solid, sound and steadfast in the Word of God with the ability to "rightly divide the Word of Truth". From online classes, various certificate programs to enrolling in singular classes at an accredited college/university, seminary or bible college, the cleric (learned men) has to be well informed in order to be an asset to the commune and the kingdom.

While there are something's that can be taught, there are others that must be possessed; character. Character can be defined as the complex of mental and ethical traits marking and often individualizing a person or simply put, the "stuff" of a person. Beyond the academia, accolades, awards and even the anointing, it is the character of the person that will speaker louder and will be the main element in the effectiveness of their influence.

Jesus warns, "Woe when all men speak well of you…" but, Woe, when NO ONE speaks well of you! Your character is the seat of your witness. If they can't believe you, then nothing you say will be accepted nor received.

Character is critically vital in leadership. As Overseers or just clergy in general, one must remember is that your character is all you have! People don't receive what they can't trust. Once your character is in question, no matter how anointed, intelligent and articulate you are people won't receive you or anything that you have to say.

The character of a leader is further discussed in Exodus 18. In Jethro's conversation with Moses, he tells him to select some men to assist him, as the work that he was doing was too much for him and by doing it alone, it would be detrimental to him and to the people. In this selection criterion, Moses (The Bishop) should select the leaders (Overseers) that have competence and character. Notice that competence is found in the singular word "able" and then there are more words attached to character. This is to denote that strength of character is held in high regard when it comes to leadership; almost more than skill itself. This is to solidify the aforementioned regarding skill vs. character.

The same is true in regards to the all to famous epistle of Paul to Titus. He records in the first chapter that more importantly than "holding fast the faithful word as been taught..." and "sound doctrine" (which are found in verse 9) is the character of the episcopos! This is not to trivialize the Word of God or the doctrine of the church, this is in the midst of a culture where the Word of God was being taught, but by individuals whose motives and methods would render them guilty of ministerial malfeasance.

It is the Word of the Lord that states that God will never take back His gift nor His calling! Which is to say that as an Overseer you can be gifted and called but, lack character! As one who is deemed the next in succession for episcopal consideration he/she shouldn't desire just to be gifted ALONE; but, to have the strength of their character to match or OUT WEIGH, their gifting. As great of a gift as preaching is, the cleric should always bear in mind that a sermon preached is impressive, but a sermon lived leaves an impression! Paul speaks to a son in the ministry in regards to the character of an overseer, that ultimately is a vital qualification! This qualification is stated in that the "testimony" of the overseer must be "good". Another Pauline epistle drives this point, is found in the seventh verse of I Timothy 3, when it is stated that the overseer's "testimony" must be "good".

While your deeds are in the moment and for the season, it is your name that will be remember in the annals of time and will be the foundation of your legacy! Hence, Solomon's wisdom concerning such in regards to reputation and the promise that God made Abram; BOTH were in regards to their NAME/CHARACTER!

It is the combination of credentials and character that cause the Overseer to be proficient in their vocation. It's not a matter of one versus the other, it is BOTH; together that enable the surety of decision and the soundness of doctrine to be made manifest in the office where which they serve. It is the character that corals the ego of the overseer, when the intellectual prowess that spawns innovative preaching and intuitive problem-solving causes internal piety. It is the credentialing that ignites and initiates the innovation of the overseer that allows the character of the Christ to be on display.

The combination of the two is the medium whereby Christ receives the glory and in the leader receives gratitude for the grace given to serve n such a humbling capacity.

CHAPTER 4

THE APPOINTMENT

The overseer ultimately works to support the office of the Presiding Prelate. The episcopacy is the highest level of ecclesiastical service, and as such should be safe guarded from the novice, the ill-prepared, and the spiritually unqualified. This is why the confirmation of the character, competence and credentials of the elder are so important as to not hinder the success of succession in the episcopal line. Oversight of special areas of ministry is then placed under the purview of these priests who have shown potential to effectively lead and administrate. This is the basis for the office of Overseer. Foremost, the Overseer is chosen by the Presiding Prelate, or at times recommended by other bishops under whom they may serve or may have a connection to in the area the overseer will oversee. It is imperative to understand, their authority is not inherent but derived from (subject to/controlled by) the Diocesan, Auxiliary Bishop and/or the Presiding Prelate.

The process begins with the observation of an elder or pastor that either the Presiding Prelate, Auxiliary or Diocesan Bishop views as a candidate for elevation to assist in the affairs of the commune. In some cases there is a calling for the credentials and testimony of the priests character to be presented to the Bishop(s).

Also, dependent upon who is observing for possible selection, there is an interview done to determine further if the priest in question is well equipped for the role.

Again, this is not in ALL communes, fellowships or reformations. Make sure you consult with your Protocol Officer or Diocesan Bishop to ensure the proper procedures and protocols are followed.

With all preliminary findings in order, a "Letter of Request" is sent from the Auxiliary or Diocesan Bishop to the Primate and/or Board (College) of Bishops. This letter will site the reasoning for such an appointment, which is to include their findings and copies of the elder's credentials. The Presiding Bishop or his/her designate will then send a "Letter of Acknowledgement" for the above stated request.

This is not just an acknowledgement of receipt but, also is if there are any questions and/or requirements that the College of Bishops or the Primate are requesting answers or more information, inclusive of a meeting with the requesting bishop or even the candidate, it is posed in this document.

After which, this is then followed by a "Letter of Appointment" inviting the candidate to the Office of Overseer. The appointment is to be understood as a document of apprenticeship in which the candidate infers further observation and training will be proposed as an overseer-designate. A growing practice currently is to designate overseers for a time of preparation for the office and responsibility they will hold.

During this time, designates should be subject to teaching in areas concerning church polity, leadership, and the episcopacy, whereas their work will be inclusive of all. The Joint College of African American Bishops offers courses of instruction to aptly equip such candidates prior to their consecration, as well as continuing education units suitable for maintaining excellence in ministry. It is profitable to note that the future episcopates of the church are often chosen from amongst these ranks, whereas through their assignments overseers have an opportunity to prove their ministry of administration, and their preparedness to support and operate in episcopal dignity and authority.

In most cases, based on the successful completion of the training criteria and observation period there is a "Declaration of the Review" which is an announcement of the findings.

Upon the blessing of the Presiding Bishop or designee, there is a "Public Service for the Overseer" which is usually held at the Holy Convocation of the Commune, Reformation or Fellowship. In some cases this service is similar to, but not equal to that of the consecration of a bishop but, on a lesser scale.

Once the public service has been completed with all appropriate documentation signed, the overseer is now ready to serve in their duly appointed capacity.

CHAPTER 5

THE FUNCTION OF THE OVERSEER

Now, that the overseer has been sanctified and sanctioned to do the work of the ministry as it pertains to his/her elevation, it is necessary to explore just what the assignment is.

The office of the overseer distinguishes two specific types: administrative and geographical. An administrative overseer is one whom oversees an area of ministry on a national or departmental level; for example the overseer of youth ministries, the overseer of the women's department or even the Adjutant General (which is the overseer of the national adjutancy. The expectation in this capacity is that the overseer will be effective and efficient in providing leadership within their sphere of influence. Whether the area is purely administrative such as the case in being an Episcopal Assistant or providing leadership to a/an department/auxiliary. This priest is to carry out the duties with precision and professionalism that "frees" the hands, head and heart of the bishop to which they are accountable to be able to concentrate on greater affairs. Within the auxiliary, the expectation is the same, however, growth and participation become the benchmarks for this overseer.

From the national women's department to the youth and young adults, the task at hand is to build a platform for ministry where the message and vision of the commune can be realized on a greater level and then disseminated back to the local congregations and communities. This level of ministry requires great leadership, communication and project management skills on behalf of the overseer. These elders must be mindful that they are both directly and indirectly responsible for that which is in their scope. The Overseer must infect and affect the hearts of those that they lead and cause effective and efficient change in their area of ministry through their submission, service and skill. Because of the national purview of administrative overseers they, in essence, have a greater degree of authority than that of geographical overseers whose authority is limited to their geographical jurisdiction.

Geographical overseers are those who are positioned in areas that lack episcopal oversight or the dioceses has a need for greater granularity in their diocesan governance. The first scenario affords the overseer the responsibility to be the Presiding Prelate's representative and emissary in that region, bringing a prelate's presence and ministry to a yet developing diocese.

In this role geographical overseers work to grow the existence and influence of the fellowship/reformation in that area, including increasing the number of churches in the communion in that region and caring for the needs of those pastors and churches in that region at the direction of the Presiding Prelate. While this priest is NOT a diocesan bishop, they are entrusted with the authority to speak on behalf of the Commune and it's Primate. This overseer, must always keep in mind that the Presiding Bishop can chose to place a Diocesan Bishop there over them even though they were the primary conduit of the voice of the reformation. The expectation in this scenario is that the level of service and loyalty would remain consistent with the expectations of the Primate for that diocese.

This case is VERY RARE, but not out of scope, so it would behoove the overseer to ensure that there is clarity in the orders and expectations. But, in the normal case, the overseer, barring any incident that would disqualify them from elevation, would be the primary candidate for episcopal consideration for that diocese.

The second scenario, although the expectation is for expansion, leadership development and administration are the same, this overseer's direct report is a diocesan bishop. The overseer is quite possibly over a district within the state. This is usually the case when there is a very large state such as California or Texas.

In both geographic schemes, the overseer is pastoring pastors and providing opportunity for the potentiality of other pastors to partner with their pontiff and primate.

Recruiting and planting are part of growth, while training and accountability are the tools of maturation of the leadership in that district or diocese. The aforementioned are the metrics of success for the geographic overseer.

It is important to note that both of these overseers have no inherent authority apart from the authority and power given to them by the Presiding Prelate. They are the tools of that office in the hands of that officer. Essentially, these tools are used to plow, pluck, prune and ultimately produce something powerful, progressive and productive that will make the Christ proud!

CHAPTER 6

THE VESTMENTS OF THE OVERSEER

Civic/Clerical/Tonsorial Attire

The most popular habit to our tradition is that of the western civic attire, which is suitable for everyday wear in public. This dress is characterized by the plain black suit, plain black shoes. Males should wear plain black socks, while females are encouraged to wear off black hosiery with their **skirts** (no pants in clerical dress for women). In public the standard would be for prelates to adorn in Black-Breast, whereas for church functions and when vesting the colored breast-front is acceptable.

In civic attire the overseer will always wear his/her cross suspended from a chain or cord and tucked into their left breast pocket. Other clerics of lower ranks may also wear a silver, never ornate, or with jewels, and never gold, suspended from a cord of no less than 40 inches. While the use of cords to identify a cleric's position is common, a standard system of colors and meanings is not in place for all ranks, in all churches, the following is a basic model:

Presiding Bishop/Bishops - Gold Chain

Overseer - Scarlet Cord or Silver Chain

Adjutant - Roman Purple Cord

Elder/Deacon - Black Cord

Acolyte - Black or White Cord

A. Yoke/Collar - Known also as he Roman Collar, or callaro.

Symbolism: The yoke of Christ, the receipt of Holy Orders, and complete submission to the work of Christ in humility and service.

B. Scarlet Pectoral Cross Cord - Pontifical Cross Cord

Symbolism: Jurisdiction of the prelate, bondage to the work of ministry and the Gospel of Jesus Christ.

Chain (Silver)

Symbolism: Bondage of service in Christ, a prisoner of the Gospel, Royal dignity and authority.

Pectoral Cross (Latin *crux pectus/pectoralis* meaning *breast/of the breast*)

Symbolism: The Passion of our Lord Jesus, a commitment to the Gospel of Christ, and the role of the Chief Defender of the Faith.

C. **English Purple/Blue Purple Shirt or Front** – The historical link to the Church of England which is the "Mother Church" of the Anglican Commune Worldwide.

   Symbolism: Jurisdiction of the prelate

D. **Black Suit** – Standard or "Classic" order without garnishments or contemporary tailorings.

   Symbolism: Servanthood, humility, self discipline and the dying to the flesh.

Choir Dress/Ceremonial Vestiture

The most commonly worn dress of our tradition is that of Choir Dress, so named because of its use in the "choir" area of the chancel, during the daily prayers and offices of the church, including preaching. There are some variants of choir dress for the different offices of the church, and varying practices among the different churches.

Celebration Vestments

Distinction and deference is made between the ordinary services and those of significance, in the way in which we vest. Whenever there is an ordination or consecration service, a high Holy Day or services where a sacrament of the church is being celebrated, clerics will adorn in what is known as celebration vestments.

A. **Yoke/Collar** - Known also as he Roman Collar, or callaro.

Symbolism: The yoke of Christ, the receipt of Holy Orders, and complete submission to the work of Christ in humility and service.

B. **Cassock** - From the French word casaque meaning long coat.

Symbolism: The servant's garment; represents humility, simplicity of heart and a commitment to service.

C. **Chimere** - From the French word chamarre and the Spanish word zamarra; a sheepskin coat or overcoat.

Symbolism: The jurisdiction of a prelate and the prophetic mantle. This symbolizes the prelate's Prophetic Office as Chief Preacher and Defender of the Faith. It is reminiscent of the prophetic mantle of Elijah, caught by Elisha.

D. **Rochet** - From the Old French, which derived from the Latin rochettus meaning coat.

Symbolism: Jurisdiction and Ecclesiastical dignity and distinction noting chief priestly authority (as it is the garment of the High Priest).

E. **Tippett/Stole** - Stole (From the Greek stolas, from the Latin orarium meaning scarf). This is also known as a Bishop's Scarf.

Symbolism: Servanthood and the priest's jurisdiction over the faithful. Also, predominantly known as the preaching scarf, it symbolizes the priest/bishop's authority and jurisdiction to preach the Gospel.

F. Cincture - Fascia (commonly known as the Sash)

Symbolism: Servanthood, integrity, chastity and one's commitment to a life devoted to Christ. It is also a symbol of the towel with which Jesus girded himself to wash the feet of the disciples.

G. Pontifical Cross Cord - Pontifical Cross Cord

Symbolism: Jurisdiction of the prelate, bondage to the work of ministry and the Gospel of Jesus Christ.

H. Chain (Silver)

Symbolism: Bondage of service in Christ, a prisoner of the Gospel, Royal dignity and authority.

I. Pectoral Cross - (Latin crux pectus/pectoralis meaning breast/of the breast)

Symbolism: The Passion of our Lord Jesus, a commitment to the Gospel of Christ, and the role of the Chief Defender of the Faith.

3 Keys to Vesting

Many communions, and even more clerics will be sure to "tailor" the standards of ecclesiastical dress to meet their needs, desires and sometimes budget; this is understandable and to be expected. However, when doing so, when considering what to wear on those occasions when there is no mandatory dress, keep the following three things in mind:

I. MODESTY & HUMILITY ARE THE GOAL!

When deciding to vest, the cleric should be sure that any variations or deviations from the "standard" or prescribed dress code are made with forethought of how the people will view you, and the Body of Christ, as you go forward as the Church's representative.

II. YOU CAN ALWAYS DRESS DOWN, NEVER UP!

As a rule, clerics of higher orders can always wear vestments of a lower order (within reason), however, clerics of lower orders may never wear the vestments of the higher orders. For example, a Bishop can wear a plain black cassock, however an elder cannot wear a roman purple cassock.

III.   BE PREPARED TO EXPLAIN YOURSELF!

When you vest you become the "church visible"; a tangible expression of the spiritual structure and life of the church. Everything you wear has a purpose and significance and you need to be prepared to educate any one who inquires of you.

BIBLIOGRAPHY

Noonan, Jr., J. (1996). *The Church Visible*. New York, NY: Penguin Books USA.

Norris, H. (2002). *Church Vestments: Their Origin and Development*. Mineola, NY: Dover Publications

Brooks, K. *Clothed In Humility; A Guide to Ecclesiastical Dress in the Anglican Apostolic Pentecostal Tradition*. Scotch Plains, NJ: Order In The Kingdom

About The Author...

 Overseer C. Sterling Davis, II is a preacher, speaker, mentor and lecturer that is well known for his critical thinking, passionate yet, prolific oratorical style that is accompanied by a humor that causes a healing laughter. The combination of the above stated and his God-given anointing to preach and teach from a revelatory, yet practical theological platform, as opposed to arguing philosophical and/or psychological -theological church issues, has strengthened and encouraged the faith of countless hearers across the globe. This is accomplished with great intentionality in order to move the listeners to a new dimension of thinking that expands the parameters of their personal relationship with Christ.

The ministry gift of God in him genuinely promotes reconciliation, redemption and relationship through revelatory reverence for/of God which brings relevance to current realities. This intense yet, intellectual approach to scripture has invigorated the intellect of people at various levels of living.

Overseer Davis humbly serves as Senior Pastor of the Renaissance Church in Houston, TX. In addition, he is the CEO of The Renaissance Group; a ministry collective that encompasses strategic planning, consulting and leadership development for churches and ministries and one of the principle overseers for The Renaissance Covenantal Consortium.

He is married to Beulah C. Davis and they have 4 children: Alesia Len, Kha'ryn Aleyah, Clinton Sterling Davis, III and Trinity Sterlynn.

Made in the USA
Charleston, SC
22 February 2013